THE PROFESSIONAL STORYTELLER

BUSINESS FOR BREAKFAST, VOLUME 3

BLAZE WARD

KNOTTED ROAD PRESS

The Beginning Professional Storyteller
Business for Breakfast, Volume 3
Copyright © 2016 Blaze Ward
All rights reserved
Published 2015 by Knotted Road Press
www.KnottedRoadPress.com

ISBN: 978-1-943663-06-4

All rights reserved. Except for brief quotations in critical articles or reviews, the purchaser or reader may not modify, copy, distribute, transmit, display perform, reproduce, publish, license, create derivative works from, transfer or sell any information contained in this book without the express written permission of Leah Cutter or Knotted Road Press. Requests to use or quote this material for any purpose should be addressed to Knotted Road Press.

Disclaimer

This book is provided for general educational purposes. While the author has used her best efforts in preparing this book, Knotted Road Press makes no representation with respect to the accuracy or completeness of the contents, or about the suitability of the information contained herein for any purpose. All content is provided "as is" without warranty of any kind.

Never miss a release!

If you'd like to be notified of new releases, sign up for my newsletter.

I only send out newsletters once a quarter, will never spam you, or use your email for nefarious purposes. You can also unsubscribe at any time.
http://www.leahcutter.com/newsletter/

ALSO BY BLAZE WARD

The Jessica Keller Chronicles

Auberon

Queen of the Pirates

Last of the Immortals

Goddess of War

Flight of the Blackbird

The Red Admiral

Additional Alexandria Station Stories

The Story Road

Siren

The Science Officer Series

The Science Officer

The Mind Field

The Gilded Cage

The Pleasure Dome

The Doomsday Vault

The Last Flagship

The Hammerfield Gambit

The Hammerfield Payoff

Doyle Iwakuma Stories

The Librarian

Demigod

Greater Than The Gods Intended

Other Science Fiction Stories

Myrmidons

Moonshot

Menelaus

Earthquake Gun

Moscow Gold

Fairchild

White Crane

***The Collective* Universe**

The Shipwrecked Mermaid

Imposters

INTRODUCTION

Congratulations. You have decided that you want to move beyond being just someone who writes and become a "real" writer. Hopefully, you have read Volume 1 in this series (*Business for Breakfast: Volume 1, The Beginning Professional Writer*) and now have a basic understanding of how to handle yourself, your practice, and your finances like a professional.

The goal of this book is to take a look at the basics of your craft as a (genre) fiction writer and make sure you understand what the requirements are for telling a good, professional story. Because, if you are going to act like a professional, and tell people you are one, they are going to expect these things from you. That includes, but is not limited to: editors, agents, mentors, and other professionals who will be in a position to put in a good word for you (or not, as it were).

Mind you, there are no real rules, besides making sure to have fun, but you'll sell better if people think you know what you are doing. Or if you can fake it well enough.

I didn't know these things when I was starting out. Granted, I have been a storyteller for as long as I can remember, but that didn't necessarily mean I was telling good stories. Or, to be more exact, well-crafted stories.

Sure, they were entertaining as hell, but they didn't necessarily look professional. When I decided I wanted to become a writer, both to independently publish my words and dreams and to submit to places that might pay me money, I didn't understand these things.

I got lucky. I found a mentor who laid it all out for me and basically said "Here are the bones of telling a good story. This will give you a good skeleton on which to build your stories, because the bones would be there." It wasn't everything I needed, but having it marked me as someone who was serious about the craft.

And it is a craft. Many of the writers you know are *really just playing at it*. Café dilettantes who tell you they are working on The Next Great American Novel, but they never seem to finish it. Or they write something and then tear it up because they are unhappy. They are approaching this like art.

We're going to approach this like a job. A fun job, to be sure. But a highly technical undertaking.

Within my group of friends, we call the craft "chair-making." You can make lots of different chairs, many different ways, but the end result is the same: something you can sit on. You need to follow one of many very specific methods to get a chair rather than a table, or a sofa. Knowing these will help you make a chair you are proud of.

1

THE SEVEN POINT PLOT STRUCTURE

All good fiction generally follows the *Seven Point Plot Structure*. (We're going to pretend that you can't commit literary or flash fiction without it, because the attempt often ends up wandering in the desert and never making your readers happy.) The structure has, amazingly enough, seven points to follow. They are:

1. A character
2. In a setting
3. With a problem
4. Trying
5. Failing
6. Climax
7. Denouement

The way I was taught this pattern goes back to Kristine Katherine Rusch and Dean Wesley Smith explaining how the great pulp writer Lester Dent (writer of Doc Savage, among others), banged out his stories in short order, with few re-writes, and moved on to the next one. (Something like 150+ Doc Savage novels alone over roughly 26 years, plus everything else he wrote for the various pulps under pennames. I'm told he tended to write 5000-6000 words a day when working.)

The following chapters delve into each of these points in greater detail.

For now, I want you to take a few moments to think about your favorite novel or story. It had to have worked for you, spoken to you, in order to become your favorite. Odds are, it did the same for others along the way.

The premise in fiction is really rather simple, once it is broken down. You have a main character. They can be a hero, or an anti-hero. Their job is to be the protagonist. The story rotates around their decisions.

This character exists in a setting. It might be high fantasy, low space opera, noir, western, historical, or modern. It is a place. It might be another character all by itself, depending on the story.

The main character has a problem. They *must* have a problem. It will generally start small, then grow, and turn out to be the most earth-shattering problem they have ever faced, and their whole future will turn on the outcome. Because, let's face it, who wants to read four hundred pages about a man making toast? (Don't get me wrong, I can think of a couple of writers who could do it, and have you absolutely on the edge of your seat, turning page after page and never able to put it down. You and I aren't them. At least not yet.)

So that character has a problem. It defies them. It defines them. They must do something. They try. I don't know what they try. Neither do you. They'll tell us when we get there. But they try.

And they fail. That thing they were going to do--so obvious, so simple--doesn't work. It thwarts them, laughs in their face. Dances around the room while they chase it.

So they try something else. This creates the try/fail loop. More later, but understand that the character must fail in order to succeed later.

Finally, everything builds to the climax. Our hero, repeatedly thwarted by the dastardly villainous toast, finally brings it to the peak of angst. And then, and only then, do they succeed. Without that tension, the audience feels robbed. Even if the toast is finally defeated in the end.

And then, at the very last, you bring it all to closure. If you are telling a love story, this is the happily-ever-after. If a hard-boiled detective story, the cops haul the bad guy away in cuffs. You close with a moment of "What does it all mean?" Again, happily-ever-after. Or perhaps the shamus stares into the camera and utters some utterly profound bit of wisdom about dreams or chess. That's up to you, but you need to give the reader something to bring it all home. Something that tells the reader that the story is finished.

That's it. Seven points. Pretty straightforward, all in all. But you should understand each point in order to use them like tools when making your chair. Because, people, readers, are going to look at your chair and judge you on those same criteria.

It sucks. It's unfair. But that is the way it is done. If you want to be one of the good ones, you have to, at a very minimum, be able to tell a story that recognizably fits the definition of a good chair. It could be a stool, a lounger, or an ottoman. That's up to you, because you're the one making the chair.

Good luck.

2

CHARACTER

Stories are about people. Cowboys, knights, private detectives, princesses, trolls, frogs. Your story is about someone. It is how we, the reader, identify with things in the story.

So let's talk about protagonists. Your protag is the main character. The story around whom everything else happens.

They are generally the character with whom the audience is supposed to identify. Whether or not that means they are likeable is a different story. Good writers can make the most despicable scum of a person be heroic and likeable in some way. When you get good, you can do that too.

Hamlet was a protagonist. Things happened to him, and around him, and because of him. He drove the story, even while it drove him. He was the center of things. It was a story after all, about Hamlet, the Prince of Denmark.

When making your protagonist, you need to go deep into what makes him or her tick. What are his loves? What are her fears? Why is this single piece of toast so overwhelming that we will define our entire existence on the ability to successfully crisp it, butter it, and defeat it in single combat at the breakfast plate?

You need to know these things about your protagonist. (I write copious notes when I prepare. That might not work for you, but you get to listen to my bad habits, and then figure out how to make them work for you.) Every little note you make about your character might not end up in the final draft, but the act of creating them will ensure that you have a deep and interesting character. More importantly, it will help you explain why they are going off on some bizarre tangent in a way that the audience will accept and follow.

There is nothing worse than having a character who is so unbelievable that you lose your reader. I've thrown a book across the room in the middle of the paragraph, picked it up, and sold it (and the previous three in the series) to the local used bookstore because the writer transformed the character into something else without any transition, without any explanation, nothing. (It was like a different author started writing the book at that moment. I have my suspicions.)

But there are other characters that will make up the story as well. Some of them will work to help out the hero, while others will oppose him. It is not enough to have a rich and interesting main character. Who are her friends? What makes them interesting? How, exactly, does one become a toaster repair person and make a living at it? Who rustles breakfast dragons, anyway?

You will generally need a lesser amount of depth about your supporting cast, but you should take the time to explore them. They will be way more fun as "real" people than as cardboard cut-out archetypes/tropes. Do you really need the homeless lady on the front stoop offering sage advice from the ages? Why can't it be the cute guy at the flower shop instead? Take the time. They will reward you, and they will make the story all the more interesting.

Which leads me, also, to villains. You have a protagonist. She is, as far as the audience is concerned, the hero of this tale. But a good hero is defined by the measure of the villain they face. If they face laughable, card-stock villains, you will have a laughable, card-stock melodrama. (And I will take a moment here to assume you are aspiring somewhere more than that. If not, put this book down and go back to your coloring instead.)

As much effort as you put into your hero, your protagonist, your Hamlet, your toast-maker, you need to put in at least as much to your villain. Who is it, after all, that is trying to thwart the hero? Why can't we have fresh toast this morning? Is it another person stopping us? Is it ourselves and our sense of ennui? Did Mother Nature herself get up this morning and decide she was going to torture you specifically, and decided that toast was her medium of communication? (She does that occasionally, trust me.)

Yeah, see? That's got you thinking about the other half to the story, didn't it?

Remember, the antagonist, the person who is usually the villain of the piece, they have something important to say.

Nobody gets up in the morning and says to themselves, "Today, I'm going to be the villain." (If you do, seek professional help. This book won't cover your needs.) Every villain gets up in the morning and sees themselves as the hero in their own story. Always. That's what makes them a good villain.

While we're on the topic, let's talk about Point of View (POV) for a moment. (This is generally a thing in fantasy, mystery, and science fiction. Other genres have other rules.) You are writing about a character. Good fiction lets you tell stories from various viewpoints. You can see things from the protagonist point of view, or the antagonist, or some other character, perhaps Ishmael. Rarely the great, white whale.

For the audience to stay with you as you tell your story, you need to observe a couple of strict rules about characters and Point of View.

When I write, I start every chapter or section with the name of the character from whom the point of view originates, sometimes as the first word. Usually at least the first sentence. At least the first paragraph. This POV can be third close or third universal. (If I'm in first person, that's usually obvious. And I'm not talented enough to try to write a story from multiple first person viewpoints, although I have seen it done and done well.)

So you have established your Point of View as 'Man Making Toast.' From that point until the end of the section/chapter, everything needs to remain in his point of view. What he sees. What he knows. What he thinks. What he can guess about others. If you need to get inside another character's head, that is usually the sign that you need to round off this section and switch.

Never (never never never) switch your point of view inside of a section. (Unless you are writing Literary or Romance.) Never. You lose readers that way. And it is unnecessary. When your First Reader points out a changing point of view, kiss them, apologize, and fix it. You screwed up, not them.

So, points to remember about character:

- You have a Protagonist. Make them interesting.
- You also have an Antagonist/Villain who should be AT LEAST as interesting as the hero, if not more so.
- Pay attention to your Point of View as you tell the story, so we know which character is thinking about what.

3

SETTING

So now you have a character or three (see previous chapter). And you've taken the time to make them interesting folks. Or, if you're writing into complete darkness, you keep adding things to make them interesting. Maybe they are heroic types, maybe they're loveable goofs. And you have a "villain" as well (we all know how evil toast can be when it sets its mind to it).

So now we need to talk about Setting.

Your story takes place somewhere. This is the setting. And it is just as important as the characters are, possibly more so. Let's examine why.

My teachers have often referred to Setting as the character's voice. You should give as much thought to the setting for your story as you do for your main characters, because so much of the flavor of the piece will be driven by the place they are. It might also be another character. But it's *always* the voice of the character. You don't see anything except through the eyes of the character. Therefore, everything is influenced by the character, and is described in their particular voice.

For example, a group of evil elves chasing a couple of orcs through a wet, eerie swamp is going to have an entirely different tone and feel than if they are running through a city. It's going to be dark, and damp, and shadowed in strange ways. You might run into trolls, or boars, or other wandering monsters. And there won't be anyone to help you out.

And your favorite private detective works in 1930's Los Angeles or San Francisco because those were gritty places for gritty characters and gritty tales. Dames and mugs and molls and punks. Strangers passing through. Old Money that needs something quietly resolved without involving journalists. Stolen gewgaws and ancient treasures. Plus, of course, the requisite double-cross.

For me, the best approach to setting has always been to treat it like another character. When I start my character encyclopedia (how I keep track of continuity issues), I will usually include one for the setting. If it is a bistro that will be central to the characters or the story, where is it? What other places are nearby? If I put it in a real place, like Seattle, I'll even try to walk the neighborhood to understand the flavor of the streets, or bring up a video tour on the interwebs. It makes things more immersive for me, and lets me make it more realistic for my readers.

Your Mileage Will Vary, but I strongly suggest that you go extra long and extra deep into the details, at least in your notes, when working out your thoughts on the setting. It will be rewarding.

That being said, I don't ever end up using all the details I have worked out, lest I bore the reader. But I have them, in case I want to use them later on, because I have a tendency to write serial characters, so I might need these details later, and I want them to be right.

And as an aside, I tend to come up with more details as I work. Those get put into the notes for later as well.

Here's an exercise you can do. As you start your next piece, after you have worked out your two or three main characters, try to come up with a single noun and a single adjective that describe your setting. If you plan to cover a lot of ground, you might need to do that for each major section, or possibly even each chapter. In my examples above, scary swamp or gritty city would cover a lot of it. Abandoned spaceport. Magical castle. Central Park.

The whole purpose of setting, to reiterate, is to provide a place for the characters to interact, both with each other and with the place itself. Even if it doesn't need to be any more detailed than a false-back stage, it is still worth taking the time. You never know when some little facet will open up whole new levels of the story you did not know were even there when you sat down.

This is doubly important for me, because I'm the kind of writer that writes into darkness far more than I work from a detailed outline spelling out each scene before I start to write. I'm used to suddenly getting into a scene and going "Oh, I didn't expect that. Okay," and running with it.

Use whatever techniques work best for you. Just remember that the amount of effort you put in to the setting will reward you with a more realistic place. After all, you might need to know exactly what years that particular toaster model was manufactured, so that the 1% of your audience that are experts on toasters will not lose their suspension of disbelief. And you might not need to know.

Now, the other part of a good setting is how the character feels about it. The swamp is scary because the character is scared while there. The city is a gritty, hard-scrabble place, because the character only ever sees the hard-luck cases, the people down on their luck, the grifters working their cons, and the marks falling for them.

When you describe your setting, you must filter everything through the point of view of the character talking and thinking. This is what grounds your reader in the character, makes the character more real for your reader. It might be enough to say that the barn is a faded maroon color. It's better, however, to talk about how the color of the big, ancient, two-story building reminds the character of an especially good sunset, from when they were young and in love. This connects the reader to the character and to the place.

This also helps you get the reader deeper into the character and how they think.

What have we learned:

- How the character feels about the setting, rather than just describing it.
- Treat your setting as a character and give it detail.

4

THE PROBLEM

So you have a character. You've spent a lot of time working out their likes and foibles. There is even an antagonist who might yet become the villain, given time.

And you've established a setting, whether it is a seedy New Mexico bar with a stuffed armadillo in a sombrero on the bar, or the massive wooden gate reinforced with iron that protects a fantasy fortress from evil, marauding elves (all elves are evil, just so you know). Wherever you are, you've got scenery that the characters can chew on, if necessary. A place they love or hate. Maybe it reminds them of love, or prison, or both.

Now, you need a Problem. Or rather, two levels of problems.

First you have the smaller day-to-day stuff that leads to The Problem, eventually. Think about the character trying to light her cigarette outside of the bar. Tries, fails. Goes around the corner where there's little light and less wind. Tries, fails again. Goes into the dark alley behind the bar. Still can't get her cigarette lit. Then a flame flares in the darkness. She accepts the light, looks up, realizes it's her partner. And he's dead. Hadn't even realized he was a ghost.

This is one way that small problems, everyday problems, like a rock in a shoe, can lead to the big problems.

It's not enough to get out of bed, get dressed, and go to work. Most of us do that every day, generally with a minimum amount of fuss and bitching. You need something earth-shattering.

As one of my teachers explained it once, the big problem that occurs should be the most important thing to ever happen to them. (If writing serial fiction, it is often a very important thing, like a critically-big case for a cop or private detective, but not necessarily the greatest thing ever. YMWV.)

This problem, however, must blast them completely out of their normal routine and raise the stakes to absolutely huge levels. After all, what is your morning without the perfect piece of toast?

In detective fiction, the problem is usually a dead body, and all the repercussions that come with it. For our orcs above, it's a group of angry elves coming over the rise, shooting first and not bothering to ask questions. It might even be a dead toaster that has come to represent the failure of truth, justice, and the American way, in our inability to have our correct breakfast this morning.

The importance of the problem you give your hero is to establish what is at stake. In many thrillers, it is often nothing less than the complete collapse of everything at the feet of some world-spanning supervillain's plan. In detective fiction, often someone dies, someone innocent is being framed, and someone else is going to get away with it, but for your hero.

Whatever it is, man against nature, man against man, or man against self, you need to identify the problem at hand and make sure you clearly communicate it to your readers. They need to be able to understand and appreciate it.

This will also set you up for secondary problems that are each a direct outgrowth of the main problem. Romeo is in love with the daughter of his family's enemies. And, oh, by the way, happens to kill one of them in a little brawl and start a new round of the old blood feud, until he has sharks circling him and everyone, pretty much, has to die. (Shakespeare wasn't big on happy endings. You did know that, didn't you?)

At the same time, let us not forget that a good villain will also have problems. After all, he wants to marry the princess, but she's in love with the gorgeous young hunk and wants nothing to do with the villain's power and money.

The activities of the story will revolve around each of the characters and the problems that they face. Usually, the two sides will be opposed, so they will be competing and fighting. Sometimes, they will make common cause for a while, until the inevitable falling out. But that's for later.

For now, just remember that good fiction is better when every major character faces some problem. How they overcome it, or don't, will be used to tell their story arc, to make them interesting, and show how they grow (or don't). After all, the problems can escalate radically, from one's personal world being destroyed to the entire world collapsing.

To take away:

- Every scene starts with a problem. Can be as small as tripping over the cat (again!) or as large as an earthquake about to hit LA.
- Problems generally start small and get bigger as the story expands.

5
TRY

Okay, so now we've arrived at the point of narrative fiction. We have a character, in a setting, with a problem. Your story will begin thus. In fact, every scene should start like this. Every time you have a break, reset the reader with a character, in a setting, with a problem. After all, you need to tell us the basics somehow.

Once we (the reader) understand the problem, we can start rooting for the hero to somehow solve it. After all, we're here to be entertained.

However, to tell good fiction (and not just wander around aimlessly, as is often the case with literary fiction), the hero needs to do something that they believe will solve the problem.

They must *try*.

It will not succeed. If it did, we wouldn't have a story.

No, instead, it must not work. It must fail. They must fail. But that's the provenance of the next chapter.

For now, we're going to talk about what it means to try. We have a problem.

There's no damned toast.

There are a number of things we could do to solve this problem that has so up-ended our morning that it threatens to cause our entire identity to unravel. We could check and make sure we plugged the toaster in (*oh, right, you've never made THAT mistake. Uh huh*). We could get out tools and try to disassemble the toaster in our quest to bring everything to holy centrality. We could throw the bread on the stove and toast it the old fashioned way. Whatever.

We're going to try something.

And this is where it gets tricky. After all, what we try must be an outgrowth of who we as a protagonist (or antagonist, if necessary) are. That stems from the kind of character you decided to establish in Chapter 2. If we're a forgetful schlub, checking the plug might be what it takes. Ultra-nerdy mechanical dork (or mad scientist, or both) might take the toaster apart and try to fix whatever has gone wrong with the latest invention. (After all, if the mad science inventions actually worked, he'd already be rich or emperor, depending on his bent.)

So when you try something to fix your problem, it must be something the reader would expect from the character we have already built and the setting we have put them into. After all, fixing a toaster with stone knives and bear skins only works if you have the right doctor at the right time.

As a reader, I can't stress enough how important this little facet is. As I mentioned earlier, I've thrown a book across the room and sold it and the rest of the series because the author made a monumentally huge change in how the character reacted to her world, in the middle of book four. And he had not, at any point, prepared me for the character to go through this sudden, wrenching change in her entire being. I would have been prepared to go along with it, had we moseyed up to it, sideways-like. Or telegraphed it from twenty pages out.

Nope, we just became an entirely out-of-character character.

For you, the writer, how you try to solve your problem must exist within the confines of who you as a character are. Or I'm going to need a good explanation. Or better, show them doing something in character so that when they try it later, it flows.

Say, we start out sitting in the workshop, madly tuning the broken death-ray that we will use to hold the city hostage. Weird, but establishing. Later, if I have to take a toaster apart to fix a loose coil, that's in character.

- The lesson here is that the protagonist must strive to overcome themselves, in the course of overcoming their adversary.
- Try, Try, Try. But keep it believable.

6
FAIL

So we have a problem. We can look at it analytically, or superstitiously, or however, and we try something we think will work to solve it.

Whatever the character tries must fail. Period. End of discussion.

If it had succeeded, the character would have moved on with his day. And, more importantly, learned no useful lesson. It is, after all, just toast. We have it every morning.

No, it fails. Generally, it is not a total failure. We might partially succeed.

Perhaps we've scorched the toast so badly as to make it unpalatable. But still edible. Or the bad guys have shown up and we have to blast our way out of the space port under fire, just barely making our escape. Now we're hungry, or fugitives. Or hungry fugitives; the worst kind, after all.

But we have failed. That thing that we thought would solve the problem has not done the trick, or done the wrong trick, or whatever. It has left us no closer to resolution than when we started, and often farther away.

As a corollary for good (genre) fiction, at the same time that your hero partially fails, your villain partially succeeds. They are, after all, two sides of the same coin. We have not captured the young buff stud, but we have had him declared an outlaw and him and his faithful sidekick chased into the deep woods, or the asteroid field.

And stolen his toast. It is only a matter of time before he is captured, or brought to justice. So, partial success.

From the hero's point of view, we have been declared an outlaw and hounded into the woods or asteroid field one step ahead of prison or death. Usually, in the middle of lots of arrows or explosions. ACTION stuff.

But the princess is going to marry the evil count if we can't do something to stop it. And, like, right away, even!!!

Our first attempt, to convince people he was evil, failed. He framed us. We've got to run or we'll be killed. The toast has been ruined and we're all out of bread! We are, on the surface of it, a partial failure.

But we have not totally failed. That is the important second part. Early in the story, the tries are small, and so are the fails. As we progress, the stakes get bigger. This builds dramatic tension.

You can even have the hero succeed sometimes, as long as it leaves her worse off than where she started. Like being able to successfully get the mop to start washing the floor! But now it won't stop…

To reflect this, often the fails get bigger than the tries. Think of the classical 3 Act play. As you progress out of Act 1 and get to the end of Act 2, generally, things get worse until they are just about as bad as they possibly can be. This sets you up for an Act 3 that is the titanic battle between good and evil, as the giant planet-killing monster is just about to get you, or you finally come face to face with the childhood trauma that has left you so fearful of a morning without toast.

So remember…

- Failure is *always* an option.
- Your hero must try and fail, first at the small things, like getting the rock out of his shoe, then the big things, like escaping the runaway monster truck.

7
TRY/FAIL

We've discussed what it means to try, and why it is important to fail. When you put these things together, you get what's called a try/fail loop. How long your story is, and how involved, will both dictate how many try/fail loops you have and be driven by them.

After all, you began with a try that failed. And that caused things to get worse. Then you have to try again. Try something else this time. It will work, for sure, right?

Wrong.

It fails even worse. Things keep getting wrong-er, until finally, you must face the ultimate cataclysmic confrontation (with Movie Voice Guy providing the ongoing trailer narration...)

And all the while your protagonist is trying and failing, your antagonist may be trying and succeeding, making things even worse for your protagonist.

Thus, you build dramatic tension. Nobody really wants to read a story about the guy for whom everything goes right in his life. (We all hated that kid in school, after all.) We want messy, ugly, scrambling. We want to see the little guy beaten down but never defeated, until finally he emerges victorious with toast in hand!

The way you do this is the try/fail loop.

We'll talk later about story lengths and technical definitions, so don't worry too much about it here. Instead, let's talk about the number of these loops you need. In a very short story, there might be very few, possibly only one (try, fail, try, succeed). Children's fables often work this way. After all, the tortoise didn't do much to beat the damned rabbit. He just kept trying and let the bad guy defeat himself, thus teaching us all the important lesson to trip the snarky bastard when he runs by you. (*What? That wasn't it? Oh, right. Keep your head up in the face of adversity and let slow and steady win the race. Whatever.*)

When telling longer stories, obviously you need more loops. After all, while setting can be fun, description tends to bog the reader down and eventually bore them.

They want action. They want tension.

They want the kind of paragraphs that drive you forward and make you turn the page.

It's okay to have lots of try/fails, as long as you make the story progress. (Or, alternatively, make the character progress. After all, a prisoner in a tower isn't going anywhere physically, but they can think big thoughts while being repeatedly defeated by their evil step-mom.)

Build it. Milk it. Drive it.

The purpose here is to build dramatic tension over time. Will this work? No. Okay, how about that? Crap. Will we ever have toast again???

And you are not limited to just the hero in your try/fail loops. After all, the villain has to try. His fails are usually "mostly successful" but he must keep trying to defeat the plucky hero and ruin breakfast.

One other way to also drive tension, while we're on the topic, is to use cliff-hangers. Instead of wrapping up each chapter in a happy little bow, instead leave the hero dangling, literally, from the edge of a cliff. Or have the door kicked in and then cut to a different character. We put the toast in the toaster and the entire building shorts out. Darkness. Cut. Wait. WHAT HAPPENED?

Dramatic tension, it makes you want to turn the page to see what happens next.

For example…

8

CLIMAX

See, lots of dramatic tension. It built up slowly, as different things happened. Tries failed. We tried again. We've taken apart the toaster. We've bought a new loaf of bread. We're facing the ultimate villain in the ultimate villainous show-down.

This is the Climax. Act 1 established the characters, the setting, the problem. Act 2 was all about the try/fails that drove our hero to the brink of ruin.

Now, we're fully invested in the hero, hissing at the villain, cheering for the princess to escape and find true love. Things have gotten as bad as they can get. The villain is right on the verge of winning everything, forcing the hero into one last roll of the dice.

If you have slowly and methodically escalated your tension over the course of the story, with believable characters doing crazy shit that is right in line with their skills and expertise, and never quite succeeding, and never quite failing, then your reader should be on the edge of her seat, cringing with anxiety. If you, as a writer, felt that way when you were writing it, that's a good sign. It means you are all in, fully invested, going for broke. The reader? They're right there with you, waiting to see.

Now, this is where it gets crazy important. On this last throw of the dice, the hero must succeed, and the villain must fail. Nobody has to die (unless it's THAT kind of story), but things finally turn for the hero. The winning shot lands just as the buzzer sounds. The mask falls off and reveals that old Farmer Jones was the monster the whole time. Something. It finally works this time.

The hero wins. The villain is vanquished. We have toast again.

Bonus points if the reader feels like they need a cigarette when they finish the climax. It's called a climax for a reason.

You as the writer have to pay extra special attention here. Every other try/fail failed. What is it about this try/fail that succeeds? And how have you telegraphed it to the audience that it's coming? Because you gotta prep the reader. And it is best if you do it subtly, but not so subtle that your readers are left scratching their heads.

Example of a bad climax is when the hero is just about to die and the villain about to triumph, when the gods themselves come down in their god machine, their *deux ex machina*, and fix everything. Unless the whole story originally revolved around awakening the gods so that they could fix the problem (and that's a legitimate story trope), this is usually the sign of a lazy writer or a bad ending.

They have, as the saying goes, painted themselves into a corner and can't get out in any logical manner, so they throw some ultra-powered guy in to save the day. Think of a proto-godling wizard with an English accent who just happens along whenever the heroes are in a pinch.

If your first readers tell you that you've done this, you need to apologize and fix it. Because if they think you've done it, and they like you enough to read drafts for you, the average reader is going to see it and feel betrayed. That means they won't buy your stuff in the future. Bad juju.

So bring your story to a great climax and save the day within the character's story line. If he has been developing new and exciting powers, but they have been unreliable, this time they work. Or the villain has been having problems with his own invention, and the hero manages to trap him in it. (Dude, never use lava pits to kill heroes. It never works.)

The key here is simple. You've got an entire story to build with. You want to build it to this point, this fever pitch, so you can save the day, and your toast, and leave the audience cheering. Not surly and disappointed.

It's up to you.

So remember:

- Go all in at the climax. The hero is throwing everything they have at the problem. So is the villain. It's go big or go home time.
- The hero needs to solve her own problem, not have the gods or some handy wizardling just show up and do it for her.

9

DENOUEMENT

Okay, so we've saved the day, thwarted the villain, rescued the princess. Our toast is perfect. The dramatic tension you built so carefully is done. Everybody needs a cigarette.

Now what?

In the denouement, the goal is a return to normalcy. We have come full circle to where we started, but we're better off because we've become a hero and solved a major catastrophe, however personal it might or might not be. We've got a little pocket dragon now that happily toasts the bread with her fire breath each morning, in exchange for fresh cashews and the occasional scritch between the ears.

In both romance and comedy, this is the point where the Happily-Ever-After (or, for modern readers, Happy-For-Now) comes into play. In mystery or fable, you revealed the resolution at the climax, and we learn the important lesson that crime never pays.

To put it kind of bluntly, if we follow the Shakespearean model here, and we generally should, everybody gets what they have coming. If you are a hero, good things. For the villain, defeat. For series characters, the ending might not even solve things, since a good villain should come back and plague the hero and the sidekick again. (After all, where else will a good sequel idea come from?)

And not every character needs to learn some important and

valuable lesson, although the major characters should. Some people never learn. I'm sure we all have friends who always seem to repeat the same stupid mistakes, over and over again. In the story, they might not show any development, or change, or *character arc*.

That's okay, if you understand going in that this is supposed to happen. Or it advances some other, greater, story. Or it is your theme, such as a lovelorn skunk who just won't ever take no for an answer. Comedies often end that way, after all. It makes comedic characters more fun, and keeps things light. IF THAT IS YOUR INTENT.

Otherwise, learn your lesson about how to be a better person. Discover how to better control these new powers you have. Learn how to eat a scone in the morning instead. Become someone better than you were at the beginning of the story.

But not perfect. Ye Gods, nobody wants that.

At the end, think about:

- Telling everyone that the story is over and it's time to leave.
- Order has been restored, lessons have been learned, villains have been vanquished…at least for now.

10

OPENING PARAGRAPH, CLOSING PAGE

Okay, so that's the Seven Point Plot Structure for you. Learn it. Understand it. Live it. Once you understand the rules, then, and only then, can you break them and maybe get away with it. And make morning toast exciting.

There are two other things I want to discuss: the opening paragraph and the closing page.

When someone sees your book, they first encounter the cover. Good art that accurately portrays your theme in an exciting manner while still adhering to genre is necessary. But generally out of your hands. Your publisher will put a cover on your story. (Maybe, like me, you married a fantastic graphic artist who also does awesome covers as a publisher. If you self-publish, there are books in this series to help you with the basics. I highly recommend taking the time to understand these things, because being a good writer does not automatically give you a good eye for covers. That is also a craft.)

Next, your potential reader reads the blurb. Again, usually assembled by the publisher, possibly with your input. But there is only so much you can do to make it pop without giving everything away. You only have one or two short paragraphs to work with here.

What you can control is the opening paragraph of the story. When the readers sees the cover on the shelf, or in their recommended queue, and they are intrigued, they will flip it open and read the first page.

That's it.

Let me repeat.

That's *all* a reader will look at.

You've got exactly that long to hook them. And it's not even a whole page, because usually page 1 starts in the middle. They won't turn the page unless you make them.

Everything has to be in the opening 250 words. Preferably the opening paragraph. Character. Setting. Problem. One sentence. Maybe three. Boom.

I suggest you look at those opening words you've written for existing stories again. Several times. You can't explain anything to the reader in the *second thousand* words. They won't make it there unless there is something so utterly compelling in the first *one hundred* that they have to read it.

Worse, they won't give you any money, which is really why we're all here, isn't it?

Learn to write good opening paragraphs. It is a skill, just like good dialogue or good sensory description. It can be learned. It gets you readers that turn to page 2, readers who are already excited and invested.

Once you get good enough, hours will have passed and the reader will hit the end without once coming up for air. You do that, you'll have very happy readers, merrily bitching that they literally couldn't put the book down.

That starts with the first word.

Your first words sell your current book.

Additionally, the last words of the climax and epilogue are crucial. We talked about it in the chapter on climax, but I want to reiterate it. Nothing makes a reader angrier than a bad ending. We call it "not sticking the landing."

Your last paragraph is what sells your *next* book. Give the reader a great experience, and they'll go look you up, searching for your other stories. Give the reader a bad experience and they'll toss the book to the side and never buy anything from you again.

Maybe your ending for this piece was weak, or out of character, or *deux ex machina*. Whatever. When you wrote it, did it feel right? Go with your instinct. If your brain doesn't like it, your first reader probably won't either. At that point, you have two options.

First, try to identify what it is about the ending you don't like so you can fix it. Consider re-writing parts of the ending cold.

Did you set up the ending at the beginning? Does the opening presage the closing, but not give it all away? Have you properly telegraphed what is coming to the reader, along the way?

Second, make sure you listen to your First Readers. They are invested in making the story work by volunteering to read for you. They have expectations about how you should have ended it. Expectations that are probably not going to be as emotionally wrapped up in a bad ending as yours are.

And we all do it. It's okay to let go and let your first readers suggest a better ending. If you aren't going to listen to them, why did you ask them to read for you in the first place?

The ending has to stick. When you release your story into the outer world, either by publishing it yourself or submitting it somewhere, people who are not invested in your success will be reading it and judging it, and by extension, you. Make sure what they see is the best you can do.

However, do not endlessly obsess over the opening and closings. There is an old running joke about a quote attributed to John Steinbeck (whether it is true or not is beside the point): "The book is never done, it's just sent to the printer."

When you think it is done, and have incorporated comments from your first readers, put it away. Stop revising it. Publish it, or submit it for publication. Then start the next story. Hone your craft through quantity, not obsessing endlessly on one book. Because, when you are done, you might have a great story, but it's the only story you have.

Think of it this way. You have baked a cupcake. It might be the best ever cupcake. But maybe you find a reader who wants a scone. Or a danish.

Write it. Complete it. Release it. Be done with it.

Rinse. Repeat.

Profit.

And to stride forward:

- You have a *very* short time to hook your reader. Make your first paragraph the best it can be.
- Your last paragraph helps sell your next book. Everything in between has to work as well, but make sure the last paragraph hits that rimshot.
- Then go ahead and write the next book.

11

LENGTHS

Many writers fall into a particular length as their wheelhouse for storytelling. That's natural. It is a rare talent, or a very skilled professional, who can regularly produce quality at both ends of the scale, the very short and very long tale. They take radically different skill sets. (And can be learned, by the way.)

So let's talk about the various technical definitions of story length. This will have a specific *commercial impact* on your career.

Very short pieces are under 2,000 words. This is generally referred to as *Flash Fiction*. Sometimes, professional editors will want even shorter pieces, perhaps 1,000 words as a top limit. You generally have to work very hard to craft something that compact and remain entertaining within the Seven Point Plot Structure. It can be done, and done well. It is a skill, after all, and not a birthright.

Generally speaking, a *Short Story*, the kind that a magazine, periodical, or anthology wants to publish, is going to fall between 2,000 and 6,000-7,500 words. You have to have a damned good story for them to stretch that limit at either end. More likely, they will simply reject it out of hand unless they already know your name. That's just how it is when they already have a six-foot high slush pile.

From a commercial standpoint, professional genre journals today (2016) are going to pay around six cents US per word. *Professional Rate*. That has not changed much in a long time, and will likely not change much in the near future. At 3,000 words, you can expect them to pay you $180.00 US. At 7,500, the check will be $450.00 US. In either case, not enough to live on, unless you generate several of these every month. But that is what the market pays, and that is what editors demand. Understand this as a commercial impact on your career.

A story that is more than 7,500 words and less than 17,500 is considered a *Novelette*. That is the technical term. Most publications aren't interested in something that length, unless it is part of an anthology. Often, these things used to turn into what we call "trunk stories" because in the old days you threw it in the trunk and left it there because it was too long to publish as a short story and too short to publish as a novel. In this modern era of indie publishing, you can put it up for people to buy and price it like a short story. (I do, BTW.)

I have an additional, personal distinction I make with my stories, since I generally only indie publish without going through traditional publishers. For me, if the story is longer than 10,000 words, I will try to make it individually available as a Print-On-Demand (POD) book, as well as an electronic sale. Anything under 10k isn't worth the extra effort, generally, and is likely to be wrapped up in a larger collection anyway (such as my *Beyond The Mirror* collections).

Starting at 17,500 and running to 40,000, the story is classified as a *Novella*. As with the novelette, they might be useful inside of a collection or anthology, but otherwise, traditional publishing doesn't want much to do with them these days.

A long time ago, they did. If you haunt the used book stores, you might find really cool Sci-Fi, mysteries, westerns, and other books where both sides are covers to a novella-length story that is back to back with another one. It was a good way to introduce readers to new authors, since they would often buy one story for the author they knew and liked, and end up with the other as a bonus.

They don't do that much anymore.

Finally, starting at 40,000 words, you have one (pretty important) technical definition of a *Novel*. Two or three generation ago, novels were often this short. More recently, traditional publishing has insisted that authors produce works that are at least 60,000 words, perhaps 80,000, or longer (as dictated by the contract.) Today, the median seems to be around 65,000. Melville's classic, by the way, runs a little over 210,000 words.

If you are writing professionally, you need to be aware of these definitions. As I said, they have commercial implications. Traditional publishing wants novels. Journals want short stories. There are other places that want more exotic lengths. Once you know what kind of story you like to tell, and what you are good at, you will know where to look for publication. My goal here is just to let you know what the market is currently looking for, so you can plan accordingly.

Your takeaways:

- Write the story to the length it wants to be. Then look for a market.
- Be aware that professional markets expect certain lengths.

12

UNDERSTANDING GENRE

What genre do you write in?

Trick question. Most authors don't really know what they write in until they've studied it extensively and come to some conclusions. Or have been told by their readers. And I'm not about to attempt an exhaustive summary encyclopedia that will be out of date before I finish it.

I would like to drive this point home, that no, SERIOUSLY, you, the writer, quite possibly don't have a single clue what genre you write in. Many writers don't. Or don't believe you when you tell them.

However, genre questions are for marketing, not writing. Ignore them until you have the story done. It will save your sanity.

Now that the writing is done, I want to talk about some of the larger, overarching genres, and give you some ideas of where to look and what questions to ask.

This is important because readers are on rails. When they walk into the bookstore, they ALWAYS go to the same sections of the store, generally in the same order. You do. Count your steps next time if you don't believe me.

Genre = marketing.

Fantasy and Science Fiction (both amazingly broad and squishy genres) get filed together. Mystery, in all its incarnations, frequently with Adventure. Romance. Etc.

Literary is literary. That means it really isn't a genre (unless *pretentious* is a genre). If you are committing literary, you can safely ignore most of the things I've talked about here and go tell whatever weird and interesting story you want. That's one definition of literary.

Past that, we're talking about genre. This is a shorthand for the kind of book you want to write, so that the reader can know what to expect when they pick it up. If they are expecting romance, you better give them romance. If you have chick-lit with robots, you will have angry readers, unless they know going in what to expect. (There are readers for chick-lit with robots, you know, just not many of them.)

So let's look at some of the major genres and your limitations as a writer.

One of the biggest is Science Fiction (Sci-fi, SF, etc.). Often classified with Fantasy on the bookshelf, science fiction is fiction that uses the future (either culturally or technologically) to tell an interesting story. There will be advanced technology, or lost tech, or something. Tech is big. It also trumps everything else. If you have a SF story, it doesn't matter what else you wrote. For example, an SF Romance is going to (probably) be SF, and not Romance, unless you hit every single rule of the romance story square on. (There are professionals who can do that. I'm not one of them.)

The only thing that trumps SF is Steampunk. If you write a Steampunk Romance story, it is Steampunk. Don't bother trying to convince people otherwise, just sell them on the merits of Steampunk that happens to have elements of romance.

Fantasy, the other half of the bookshelf, is just as messy. You might have classical, western European fantasy, with elves and orcs and dragons. There is likely to be magic. And swords. (Again, lost super-technology from "the ancients" means you probably have an SF story in a fantasy world, which can be fun to write. I have.)

But fantasy can also mean Urban Fantasy/Magic Realism, which today means the modern world with strange little magics in the corners. Perhaps shape-shifters, or wizards, or other strange paranormal beings, but in the everyday world you and I inhabit. Maybe sitting next to you at the bar. Think of covers featuring girls with bare midriffs and big swords.

Romance has a very (VERY) strict set of rules for what makes it an actual Romance as opposed to just a very good story with romantic elements. If you hit them all, you can call what you've written a Romance. However, understand that Romance readers are a very finicky lot and have strong expectations. If you miss and still try to classify it as Romance, you will piss them off. Try to never piss your readers off.

Thriller is probably as bad as Romance with prescription, but exerts a looser control. Romance has rules at every point (beginning, middle, ending) while Thriller has to start a certain way and run a certain rough path, but can vary more in the back half. Again, you can write a thrilling story without being a Thriller (often called a pulse-pounder in those circumstances). Like Romance readers, Thriller readers have tight expectations and little forgiveness.

Mystery is a much more interesting kind of story. You have a problem at the beginning, often a crime or related to one. The audience may see everything or perhaps only as much as the sleuth. And the ending is tricky. You don't have to *solve* the crime, but you absolutely must *resolve* the situation. Done well, it is an absolute nail-biter or page-turner. Done silly, it is a Saturday morning cartoon featuring a dog. Not necessarily a bad thing.

Western is more of a setting than a genre. It is that place in the late Nineteen Century American West (generally; you can do it other places) with cowboys, indians, exploration, and the growth of manifest destiny. Into that, you can put a thriller, or a romance, or a mystery. But when you say Western, your audience will immediately leap to conclusions of setting. Best that you meet them, and then you can add a genre atop your western. For example, the sub-genre intersection of Western and Steampunk is known as *Weird West*.

Horror is more of a type of story than a genre, per se. It is something really scary, but it might be vampires and it might be runaway robots. You are not restricted to the type of horror story, but it will tend to trump other things. And it sells really well, because a good scare is something people like, within the confines of being able to put the book down and walk away.

Historic is a shorthand for something grounded (however loosely) in our world's history, with or without magic added in. (Think urban fantasy in the 12th century, for example.) Anything can be historic, it is generally just the first word in your description, such as "historic fantasy set in Tang Dynasty China." You should expect to either have to know the topic well or to research it well, and then expect to eventually run into someone who is an expert. Hopefully, you are accurate enough to satisfy them. Consider recruiting them as a First Reader.

Finally, Regency period is another thing that is more a setting than a genre, although it tends to have Romance elements in it, if not to be full-on Romance by prescription. It will fall roughly into the late 18th and early 19th Century United Kingdom. People who write here are generally experts. So are their readers.

Mind you, these are just some of the bigger and better known categories. Go research what you like to read and what you think you write and see what else you need to know.

So remember:

- Chances are that you, the writer, don't know what genre you write in. Or what genre a specific piece is in. Get someone else to read it and tell you what shelf they'd expect to find this book on in a bookstore.
- Genre definitions do not matter while you're writing. Write whatever it is that you want to write. Worry about genre, and the marketing of your story, after you finish writing it, not before.
- Genres have loose definitions that change over time. What was once called "crime fiction" is now mystery, etc. Keep yourself educated on the trends in genre.

13

IN CONCLUSION...

So, that's the Seven Point Plot Structure as I learned it. You have a character, in a setting, with a problem. They try. They fail. It builds to a climax. We have denouement.

I have seen it presented other ways. It has often been attributed to Lester Dent as the originator. Various writers and instructors teach it different ways.

It is the basis of what you need to know to tell good stories that is generally recognized as such by other professionals.

Like me, you will be good at some things and weak at others. We know these things. We work them out in our writing, so we can get better. We practice.

Like me, you will write good stories and not so good stories. Some of them just won't work. That's okay. Figure out why, learn from it, and move on.

I used to have a boss that always said "Fail originally." It was okay to screw up. It was not okay to screw up the same way a second time. Then you haven't learned anything from your own try/fail cycles.

But, most important, write it, finish it, release it.

That's all I ask.

READ MORE!

Be sure to pick up the other books in the Business for Breakfast series!

The Beginning Professional Writer
The Beginning Professional Publisher
The Beginning Professional Storyteller
The Intermediate Professional Storyteller
Business Planning for Professional Publishers
The Healthier Professional Writer
The Three Act Structure

ABOUT THE AUTHOR

Blaze Ward writes science fiction in the Alexandria Station universe: The Jessica Keller Chronicles, The Science Officer series, The Doyle Iwakuma Stories, and others. He also writes about The Collective as well as The Fairchild Stories and Modern Gods superhero myths. You can find out more at his website www.blazeward.com, as well as Facebook, Goodreads, and other places.

Blaze's works are available as ebooks, paper, and audio, and can be found at a variety of online vendors (Kobo, Amazon, iBooks, and others). His newsletter comes out quarterly, and you can also follow his blog on his website. He really enjoys interacting with fans, and looks forward to any and all questions-even ones about his books!

Never miss a release!

If you'd like to be notified of new releases, sign up for my newsletter.

I only send out newsletters once a quarter, will never spam you, or use your email for nefarious purposes. You can also unsubscribe at any time.

http://www.blazeward.com/newsletter/

ABOUT KNOTTED ROAD PRESS

Knotted Road Press fiction specializes in dynamic writing set in mysterious, exotic locations.

Knotted Road Press non-fiction publishes autobiographies, business books, cookbooks, and how-to books with unique voices.

Knotted Road Press creates DRM-free ebooks as well as high-quality print books for readers around the world.

With authors in a variety of genres including literary, poetry, mystery, fantasy, and science fiction, Knotted Road Press has something for everyone.

Knotted Road Press
www.KnottedRoadPress.com

www.ingramcontent.com/pod-product-compliance
Lightning Source LLC
Chambersburg PA
CBHW070036040426
42333CB00040B/1692